Population Policies for a New Economic Era

Lester R. Brown

Worldwatch Paper 53
March 1983

Financial support for this paper was provided by the United Nations Fund for Population Activities. Sections of the paper may be reproduced in magazines and newspapers with acknowledgment to Worldwatch Institute.

The views expressed are those of the author and do not necessarily represent those of Worldwatch Institute and its directors, officers or staff, or of the United Nations Fund for Population Activities.

Table of Contents

Introduction

After a generation of unprecedented economic growth, averaging over 4 percent per year, the world economy appears to be losing momentum. From 1979 to 1982 growth averaged only 1.6 percent per year.[1] Economic analysts describe this recent stretch of slow growth as the longest recession since the thirties, but it may inaugurate a basic shift in the world economy, a shift to slower long-term economic growth.

Double-digit inflation, high interest rates and soaring budget deficits are often cited as the causes of the global economic slowdown, but these are more symptom than cause. More fundamental is the depletion of the global resource base that allowed the economy to triple during the century's third quarter. This depletion of resources, both renewable and nonrenewable, is undermining the long-term potential for rapid, sustained economic growth.

If the world economy cannot resume the robust growth of earlier years, those in countries unable to get the brakes on rapid population growth may find their incomes falling. The World Bank has reported that during the seventies economic growth fell behind population growth in 18 countries containing 121 million people.[2] In the absence of more effective family planning programs, the ranks of these countries seem certain to swell during the eighties.

Oil played a central role in the century's third-quarter economic boom. Between 1950 and 1973 yearly world oil production increased from less than four billion barrels to over 20 billion. This record growth in oil output, and the associated growth in natural gas, fueled a record growth in world economic output. With the production of this remarkably versatile, easily transportable fuel moving to a new high each year from 1950 to 1973, the energy needed for economic growth was abundant and inexpensive. At less than $2 a barrel, capital expenditures on the energy needed to expand economic output were minimal. The world output of goods and services increased by over 4 percent per year, generating a rising economic tide that raised living standards everywhere.[3]

I am indebted to my colleague Edward Wolf for his assistance with the research and analysis underlying this paper.

6 In addition to making overall economic growth easy, cheap oil revolutionized agriculture, spawning spectacular gains in food output. Although the frontiers of agricultural settlement had largely disappeared by mid-century, world grain output doubled between 1950 and 1973. This unprecedented doubling of the world grain harvest during a 23-year span raised output per person 31 percent and improved diets throughout the world.[4]

The key to this record growth in food output was chemical fertilizer, based on oil and natural gas. Between 1950 and 1973 the world's farmers increased their use of chemical fertilizer fivefold, closely paralleling the fivefold increase in world oil production during the same period.[5]

Cheap oil not only removed the cropland constraints on food production, but also acted as a safety valve as pressures mounted on the earth's biological systems. Many oil-based synthetic materials could be substituted for natural materials, just as fertilizer substituted for cropland. Synthetic fibers were substituted for natural fibers. Synthetic rubber production eventually exceeded that of natural rubber. Plastic replaced paper in the packaging industry. As land near Third World cities was deforested, kerosene was substituted for firewood. Cheap, abundant oil pushed back the resource constraints on economic expansion.

Growth in the production of oil slowed after the 1973 oil price increase and then came to a halt in 1979 after the second major oil price hike. Since then oil production has been declining, as has oil refining and the production of petroleum products. Closely tied to oil, automobile production, the world's major manufacturing activity, has also been declining steadily since 1979.[6]

Growth in other basic economic activities has slowed because of rising oil prices, because of deteriorating biological systems, or both. Affected by both rising oil prices and soil erosion, growth in grain output, averaging 3.1 percent per year from 1950 to 1973, has fallen to less than 2 percent per year since then. With overfishing now commonplace, growth in the world fish catch, averaging 6 percent per year from 1950 to 1970, has fallen to less than 1 percent during the dozen years since. The steady postwar growth in beef production came to a halt in 1976, as more and more of the world's ranchers reached the productive limits of their grazing lands. Growth in world output of forest products, rising in some regions and falling in others, had fallen behind population growth by 1970.[7]

7

As world population moves toward five billion, humanity is moving into uncharted territory. The relationship between population size and the sustainable yield of the earth's biological resource systems is uncertain and sometimes unpredictable. With the progressive depletion of readily accessible oil and gas reserves and the widespread deterioration of the economy's biological support systems, economic growth has slowed markedly.

These new economic trends call for dramatic shifts in population policy to avoid declines in consumption levels. Political leaders in a few countries have already begun to grasp this. Unfortunately, all too many have not.

Oil and Carrying Capacity

Our age is often referred to as the nuclear age, or the space age. Scientifically glamorous though these labels may be, it is petroleum that has shaped our time. The consumption of vast quantities of oil, some 60 million barrels a day at the peak of the oil age during the late seventies, gives contemporary society its distinctive character.[8]

At its peak, oil and its companion fuel, natural gas, accounted for two-thirds of world commercial energy use. Oil was the source of virtually all the world's transportation fuel, much of the fuel for heating buildings and water, and for generating electricity, and together with natural gas, it supplied most of the feedstocks for synthetic chemicals.

The fivefold growth in world oil production between 1950 and 1973 greatly outpaced population gains, sharply raising oil production per capita. (See Table 1.) This enormous growth in the use of oil sharply increased the earth's carrying capacity—the number of people the earth could support at a given consumption level. Nowhere is oil's impact on carrying capacity more evident than in agriculture, where oil-based technical advances after World War II led to unprecedented improvements in crop yields.

From the beginning of agriculture until World War II, productivity edged upward only slowly, sometimes remaining static for long

Table 1: World Oil Production, Total and Per Capita, 1950-82

Year	Oil Production	Population	Oil Production Per Person
	(billion barrels)	(billions)	(barrels)
1950	3.8	2.51	1.5
1955	5.6	2.74	2.0
1960	7.7	3.03	2.5
1965	11.1	3.34	3.3
1970	16.7	3.68	4.5
1971	17.7	3.75	4.7
1972	18.6	3.82	4.9
1973	20.4	3.88	5.3
1974	20.5	3.96	5.2
1975	19.5	4.03	4.8
1976	20.9	4.11	5.1
1977	21.8	4.18	5.2
1978	22.0	4.26	5.2
1979	22.7	4.34	5.2
1980	21.7	4.42	4.9
1981	20.4	4.50	4.5
1982	19.3	4.58	4.2

Source: Derived from U.N. demographic data and U.S. Department of Energy oil production data.

stretches of history. Rice yields in nineteenth century Japan, for instance, were only marginally higher than those obtained during the fourteenth century. U.S. corn yields during the 1930s were no higher than those during the 1860s, the first decade for which reliable yield estimates are available.[9]

9

Before 1950, increases in food output came largely from expanding cultivated area, but with cheap chemical fertilizer this changed. In 1950 farmers used 14 million tons of energy-intensive chemical fertilizer. In 1982 they used 117 million tons.[10] In effect, as fertile land became harder to find, farmers learned to substitute energy, in the form of chemical fertilizer, for land. Fertilizer factories replaced new land as the principal source of growth in food production.

After World War II crop yields rose in a sustained fashion in virtually every industrial country. Beginning in the sixties new fertilizer-responsive varieties of dwarf wheat and rice boosted food output per hectare in Third World countries—the so-called "Green Revolution." Between 1950 and the first OPEC oil price hike in 1973 the rise in cereal yield per hectare was one of the steadiest and most predictable trends in the world economy, increasing at an average of 2.2 percent annually. Overall, world grain output during this period jumped from 631 to 1,290 million tons. Grain production per capita increased from 248 to 324 kilograms, a gain of nearly one-third. (See Table 2.)

Since 1973 per capita grain production has shown little improvement, averaging 325 kilograms over the nine-year span. On the supply side, rising fuel and fertilizer costs, along with soil erosion, have all contributed to the slower growth in food output. On the demand side, the marked reduction in income growth since 1973 has dampened growth in food demand.[11]

The slower growth in overall food production has undermined efforts to raise food production per person. After the oil price increase of 1973, the annual growth in world grain production was cut by a third, from 3.1 percent to 2 percent. Before the first oil price hike, world grain output per person had been rising more than 1 percent per year, but since then it has barely kept pace with world population growth.[12]

Table 2: World Grain Production, Total and Per Capita, 1950-82

Year	Grain Production (million metric tons)	Population (billions)	Grain Production Per person (kilograms)
1950	623	2.51	248
1955	751	2.74	274
1960	804	3.03	277
1965	922	3.34	276
1970	1,099	3.68	299
1971	1,199	3.75	320
1972	1,167	3.82	305
1973	1,258	3.88	324
1974	1,219	3.96	308
1975	1,245	4.03	309
1976	1,356	4.11	330
1977	1,338	4.18	320
1978	1,463	4.26	343
1979	1,422	4.34	328
1980	1,418	4.42	321
1981	1,490	4.50	331
1982	1,523	4.58	332

Source: United Nations and U.S. Department of Agriculture.

Today, with little fertile land awaiting the plow and over 70 million additional people to feed each year, farmers everywhere are turning to energy-based improvements in land productivity to raise food output. The substitution of energy for land is graphically evident in the trends since mid-century. (See Figure 1.) In 1950, when world population totaled 2.51 billion, the harvested area of cereals per person was .24 hectares. As growth in population greatly outstripped that of cultivated area, the area per person fell steadily, declining to .16 hectares by 1982. As the amount of cropland per person declined, the fertilizer consumption per person increased, climbing from just over five kilograms in 1950 to 26 kilograms in 1982.[13]

11

With population projected to continue growing to the end of the century and beyond, cropland per person will continue to decline and the fertilizer use per person needed even to maintain consumption levels will continue to rise. At some point biological constraints on

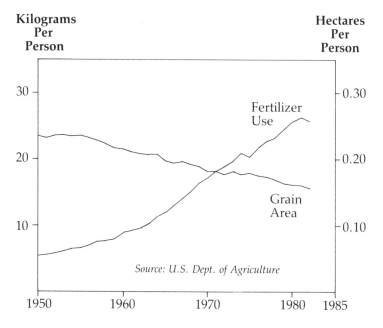

**Figure 1: World Fertilizer Use and Grain Area
Per Person, 1950-82**

crop yield per hectare of land will make the substitution of fertilizer for cropland increasingly difficult and costly. When this is combined with the projected long-term rise in real costs of the oil and natural gas used to manufacture fertilizer, the difficulty in restoring the upward trend in per capita grain production that prevailed from 1950 to 1973 is apparent.

In addition to fertilizer-based productivity gains, cheap oil boosted world food output in several other ways. Between 1950 and 1973 the area of irrigated land more than doubled.[14] As with the use of chemical fertilizer, irrigation is energy intensive. Petroleum-based insecticides and fungicides helped protect crops from insects and diseases. Mechanized tillage operations made possible by cheap liquid fuel also contributed to the growth in world food output. Virtually every major innovation that boosted food output was tied to oil.

As tractors replaced draft animals, the limits of food production expanded just as they had when farmers substituted fertilizer for cropland. Not only did mechanization help raise yields, but tractors running on gasoline and diesel fuels eliminated the need for feedgrains and forage on which the draft animals depended. Where agriculture has been mechanized, oil has in effect been substituted for land that once produced feed for draft animals. In the United States alone some 60 million acres of cropland producing grain and forage for horses were released for other purposes as tractors replaced horses.[15]

As fertilizer replaced new cropland and tractors replaced draft animals throughout the world, kerosene was substituted for firewood in Third World villages and cities, reducing demands on local forests. This substitution was encouraged by low kerosene prices and rising firewood prices as forests receded from fast-growing Third World cities.

In the laboratories of advanced industrial societies, scientists developed new petroleum-based synthetic materials to substitute for natural materials. Synthetic fibers, for example, were substituted for cotton, wool and other natural fibers. The new fibers were low-cost and in some ways superior to natural fibers. In 1950 synthetic fibers

"In 1981, replacing synthetic fibers entirely with cotton would have required an additional 23 million hectares of land."

Table 3: World Production of Natural and Synthetic Fibers, 1950-82.

Year	Natural Cotton	Wool	Cellu-losic	Syn-thetic	All Fibers	Synthetic Share of Total
	(million metric tons)					(percent)
1950	6.7	0.9	1.6	0.1	9.3	1.1
1955	9.6	1.0	2.3	0.3	13.2	2.3
1960	9.7	1.4	2.6	0.7	14.4	4.9
1965	12.0	1.5	3.3	2.1	18.9	11.1
1970	11.7	1.6	3.4	4.7	21.4	22.0
1971	13.0	1.6	3.5	5.6	23.7	23.6
1972	13.7	1.6	3.6	6.4	25.3	25.3
1973	13.8	1.5	3.7	7.6	26.6	28.6
1974	14.1	1.4	3.5	7.5	26.5	28.3
1975	11.8	1.5	3.0	7.4	23.7	31.2
1976	12.4	1.5	3.2	8.6	25.7	33.5
1977	14.0	1.5	3.3	9.2	28.0	32.9
1978	13.1	1.5	3.3	10.0	27.9	35.8
1979	14.3	1.5	3.4	10.6	29.8	35.6
1980	14.3	1.6	3.2	10.5	29.6	35.5
1981	14.4	1.6	3.2	10.7	29.9	35.6
1982*	14.5	1.6	3.2	10.2	29.5	34.6

*Preliminary.
Source: U.S. Department of Agriculture and Textile Economics Bureau.

accounted for only 1 percent of fiber use. But by the time world oil production peaked in 1979, their share had climbed to 36 percent. (See Table 3.) By comparison, cotton had a 48 percent share, wool had

5 percent and rayon, a fiber produced largely from wood pulp, had 11 percent. Overall, roughly a third of the clothing worn by the earth's 4.5 billion inhabitants is now made of fibers not found in nature.[16]

14 Synthetic fibers have reduced pressure on cropland below what it would otherwise have been. In 1981, replacing synthetic fibers entirely with cotton would have required an additional 23 million hectares of land. Although this represents only 1.9 percent of the world's cropland, its potential output is proportionately greater because cotton is grown largely on irrigated land. Planting that land with grain, assuming only average productivity, would feed 86 million people.[17]

Plastics, synthesized from petroleum and natural gas, have been widely substituted for wood, paper, cardboard, leather and other natural materials. In packaging alone, the use of plastics in the United States totaled four million tons in 1978, or some 18 kilograms per capita.[18] Increasingly plastics have replaced wood in the building, furniture, home appliance and houseware industries. As demand for leather, tallow and other livestock products used by industry has grown, oil-based synthetic materials have reduced pressure on grasslands. In much of the world synthetic detergents have replaced tallow-based soap. And as demand for leather increasingly outstrips supply, footwear and leather goods industries have turned to synthetic materials produced by the petrochemical industry.

With rubber, the substitution of synthetics produced by the petrochemical industry has progressed even further than with fibers. Although world production of natural rubber has kept pace with population growth since 1950, it has fallen far behind affluence-spurred demand. By 1978 synthetic rubber accounted for over two-thirds of the world's rubber supply.[19]

This use of oil and natural gas in the form of fertilizer, kerosene, tillage fuels and as synthetic substitutes for natural materials has served as a safety valve, alleviating the pressures on the economy's biological support systems. Plentiful supplies of oil and gas and a vast petrochemical industry keep the safety valve open. But as reserves of oil and gas dwindle, the safety valve will tighten, reversing the substitution process and putting even more pressure on cropland and the basic biological systems.

"If the entire world consumed oil at the 1980 U.S. rate of 30 barrels per person annually, proven reserves would be exhausted in five years."

The Oil Prospect

Since peaking in 1979 at 22.7 billion barrels just before the second oil price hike, world oil production has fallen each year. Production in 1982 was 19.3 billion barrels, down 15.4 percent within a three-year period. In per capita terms, world oil production fell from 5.2 barrels in 1979 to 4.2 barrels in 1982. Each of us is using an average of one-fifth less oil for transportation, heating, producing food and other uses than we did three years ago.[20] Although consumption levels vary widely among countries, the great majority are affected by the downturn. Industrial societies are making heavy cuts in oil use; developing countries will never have an abundance of cheap oil to fuel their development.

15

The age of oil will of necessity be short-lived. Indeed, the long-term decline in oil production that signals the eventual end of the oil age has already begun. Both the amount of oil used and its share of the global energy budget have almost certainly peaked. Although world oil output is never likely to regain the 22.7 billion-barrel-level of 1979 and will undoubtedly be lower at the end of the century than in 1983, there may be temporary upturns from time to time. Given the precipitous 15 percent decline from 1979 to 1982, caused in part by economic recession, even a modest global economic recovery could lead to a temporary upturn in oil production. These shortlived upturns notwithstanding, the oscillations will be around a long-term trend of falling output.

Ultimately, the days of the oil age are numbered by the size of the remaining reserves. Proven reserves of oil, those that can be extracted easily using the natural pressure in oil-bearing geological formations, total some 650 billion barrels. Estimates of ultimately recoverable reserves, a far larger category that includes expected new discoveries and allows for the use of secondary and tertiary recovery techniques and advances in extraction technology, converge around 2000 billion barrels, or 440 barrels per person for the 4.5 billion people in the world today. If the entire world consumed oil at the 1980 U.S. rate of 30 barrels per person annually, proven reserves would be exhausted in five years. Unlikely though this is, it does illustrate the finite dimensions of the oil age.[21]

16 If oil and gas production were constrained only by physical limits, output could increase sharply in the near term. But powerful economic, political and psychological forces are also at work. Oil prices already keep many countries from using as much oil as they once did. High oil prices have both spurred the substitution of other fuels and made investments in conservation measures profitable. World oil production declines in the early eighties are the result of price-induced conservation, the substitution of other fuels for oil, and the economic slowdown that has gripped the world during this period. Oil industry analysts attribute roughly two-thirds of the reduction to conservation, including substitution, and one-third to economic recession.[22]

The psychological influences on oil production are more difficult both to measure and project. As oil producing countries find their reserves shrinking as their production of oil consistently exceeds new discoveries, they often develop a "depletion psychology." The urge of countries to postpone the day when the wells go dry could steadily lower world oil production in the late eighties and nineties. The market impact of the basically healthy fear of using up an irreplaceable resource is hard to gauge. But just as the changing market psychology drove prices far above the levels projected for the seventies, a depletion psychology could markedly reduce oil production below the levels commonly projected for the remainder of this century.

Political disruptions, particularly in the Middle East, are also influencing production levels. Future conflicts involving oil-producing countries are almost as inevitable as are politically motivated oil export embargoes. Political and economic uncertainties added to a depletion psychology are enough to humble even oil experts who attempt to predict future oil production. Nevertheless, common sense suggests that in order to extend petroleum's lifetime as long as possible production in the near term should fall. The key question is whether the long-term decline in world output will be gradual and orderly or irregular and disruptive.

Production in several major oil-producing countries has already begun to decline, both because reserves are dwindling and because producers are trying to stretch out remaining reserves. Oil production in Venezuela has fallen nearly 40 percent from its 1970 high of 3.7 million barrels per day. Production reached a high in the United States in 1970 and in Canada in 1973. Other major producing countries experiencing more recent declines include Algeria, Iraq, Iran and Kuwait. With production in the Soviet Union now peaking and North Sea output slated to peak in a matter of years, substantial increases are expected in only a few countries, notably China and Mexico.[23]

17

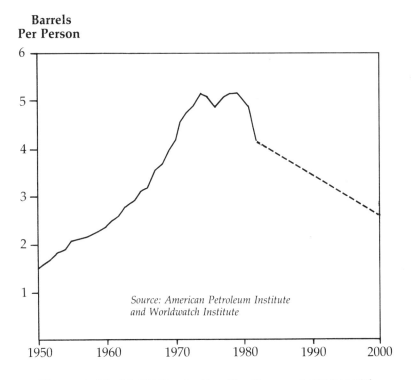

Figure 2: World Oil Production Per Person, 1950-82 With Projections to 2000

18

The combination of physical, economic and psychological factors is likely to reduce end-of-century oil output well below the current level. A continuation of the 5 percent annual decline from 1979 to 1982 is obviously highly unlikely. But a further decline of at least 15 percent between now and century's end does not seem unlikely, given the long-term output declines now under way in most producing countries. If world oil output does decline only another 15 percent by the year 2000, and projected population increases materialize, production will fall to 2.6 barrels per person. (See Figure 2.) In effect, each person would have only half as much oil as at the peak of the oil age in 1979.

A 15 percent decline would put end-of-century world oil production at 16.3 billion barrels per year, down from 22.7 billion barrels in 1979. With a decline in oil output of this magnitude the further substitution of oil-derived synthetics for natural materials and resources will become more difficult. In some situations the substitution process may be reversed.

The dramatic rise in per capita fertilizer use since 1950 has been temporarily halted in the early eighties. Whether the exceptionally rapid growth prevailing up until 1979 will be resumed over the rest of this century remains to be seen. If it is not, then regaining a food production growth rate that is fast enough to raise per capita food output will be difficult unless population growth slows markedly.

With higher oil prices, the substitution of kerosene for firewood that was proceeding rapidly in most Third World countries before 1973 has now become far more difficult. At the national level, oil-deficit low-income importing countries have curbed oil imports because of foreign exchange shortages. At the personal level, soaring kerosene prices have pushed this cooking fuel beyond the range of many low-income consumers in Third World villages and cities.[24]

As the price of oil climbed above $30 per barrel in 1979, the increase in substitution of synthetic fibers for natural fibers came to a halt. After climbing from 22 to 36 percent between 1970 and 1978, the synthetic share of world fiber output has not increased at all. Whether the substitution trend will be regained remains to be seen.

The substitution of synthetic rubber for natural rubber leveled off at just under 70 percent following the 1973 oil price hike.[25] The leveling off reflects not only the rising cost of this petrochemical product, but also the complementarity of natural and synthetic rubber in such products as radial tires. In either case, synthetic rubber's share may not increase much further, meaning that any growth in world rubber demand will translate into additional demand for natural rubber.

19

The Changing Economic Context

For most of humanity the century's third quarter was a period of unprecedented prosperity. World output of goods and services, expanding 4 percent or more annually, tripled in less than a generation. Growth had become commonplace—something that was built into consumer aspirations, earnings projections of corporations and revenue expectations of governments. Few stopped to calculate that a 4 percent rate of economic growth, if sustained, would lead to a fiftyfold expansion in a century. And even fewer considered the pressures this would put on the earth's resources, both renewable and nonrenewable.[26]

At 4 percent per year, economic growth exceeded that of even the fastest growing populations. Overall, global economic growth was more than double that of population growth, and from mid-century to 1973, living standards rose throughout the world.

Cheap energy quite literally fueled this record economic expansion of the postwar period. Oil, a versatile and readily transportable fuel, can equally well generate electricity, power machinery and serve as a chemical feedstock. Because cheap oil played such a central role in the economic boom, the dramatic price jumps of the seventies had a pervasive effect on overall economic growth. All economic activity requires energy, but at $2 per barrel, oil was a minuscule cost in the production of goods and services. At $30 per barrel billions of investment dollars are drained off, leaving less capital to underwrite economic expansion.

Table 4: Basic World Economic Indicators at Three Oil Price Levels, 1950-82

Period	Oil Price Per Barrel	Oil Production	Grain Production	Automobile Production	Gross World Product
	(dollars)	annual change (percent)			
1950-73	2	7.6	3.1	5.8	5.0
1973-79	12	2.0	2.1	1.1	3.5
1979-82	34	−5.7	1.8	−5.3	1.6

Source: American Petroleum Institute, U.S. Department of Agriculture, Motor Vehicle Manufacturers Association, U.S. Department of State and Worldwatch Institute.

The oil industry itself is a major part of the world economy. As oil demand drops because of high prices, world economic growth is slowed by downturns in oil production and refining, petrochemical production, and the marketing and distribution of oil and petrochemicals. When oil production is declining rather than expanding, those industries closely tied to oil find it difficult to grow. Of these, none has been hit as hard as the automobile industry, the world's largest manufacturing industry. Between 1950 and 1973 world automobile production expanded by 5.8 percent per year. With oil averaging $12 a barrel between 1973 and 1979, the growth in automobile production slowed markedly to just over 1 percent per year. (See Table 4.) When the world oil price was pushed to over $30 in 1979 the slowdown in production became a decline, with output falling from 31 million automobiles in 1979 to 27 million in 1982. Occasional modest upturns in world auto output are likely between now and the end of the century, but the long-term trend is unquestionably downward, a sharp contrast to the robust growth of the 1950-73 era.[27]

As automobile output declines, auto parts and machine tool industries, as well as those supplying raw materials—steel, rubber and glass—are also affected. Downturns in these basic industries have contributed to the economic growth slowdown in all the world's leading industrial societies.

"Not only have energy-intensive
agricultural inputs become more costly,
but returns on the use of additional
fertilizer are diminishing."

As oil prices have climbed, as new cropland has become scarce and as soils have eroded, growth in world food output has slowed. The annual growth in grain production, for example, has declined by a third since 1973. Given the basic role of agriculture in the world economy, this slower agricultural growth has measurably slowed overall economic growth. The effects go far beyond agriculture itself, slowing growth in the food processing and marketing industries as well.

21

Efforts to expand food production involve cultivating additional land or increasing the output on existing croplands. But farmers are beginning to experience diminishing returns in both directions. In countries as diverse as sparsely populated Canada and densely populated China, the quality of newly plowed land is far below that of settled lands. In Canada an estimated 233 hectares of new cropland in the western provinces is required to replace each 100 hectares of top-quality land lost to urban spread in the east.[28] In China the problem is even worse. Lesley T. C. Kuo, a specialist on Chinese agriculture, reports that "The use of one acre of cultivated land for construction purposes must be offset by the reclamation of several acres of wasteland."[29]

In attempting to boost grain output during the sixties and seventies the Chinese expanded their cultivated area, but much of the newly plowed land would not sustain cultivation. To correct this problem China has pulled back from the marginal lands, reducing its cultivated area by about 6 percent between 1978 and 1982. Experience in the Soviet Union, another major world food producer, parallels that in China. Since 1978 the area planted to grain in the Soviet Union has fallen by 5 percent. Both of these nonmarket economies have discovered that eventually the returns on investment in cultivated land expansion will fall sharply.[30]

At the global level, a similar phenomenon is developing with the expanded use of chemical fertilizer. Not only has this energy-intensive agricultural input become more costly, but returns on the use of additional fertilizer are diminishing, particularly in agriculturally advanced countries. Worldwide, the trend is unmistakable. During the fifties, the application of an additional ton of fertilizer yielded 11.5 tons of additional grain; during the sixties the fertilizer/grain response ratio was 8.3 to 1. By the seventies it had fallen to 5.8. (See Table 5.) Some countries, such as Argentina and India, still apply little fertilizer, and response ratios are quite high. But the worldwide return on the use of additional fertilizer is diminishing. Although the biological constraints on fertilizer responsiveness can be pushed back with continued plant breeding, further declines seem inevitable.

Table 5: World Grain Production and Fertilizer Use

Period	World Grain Production*	Increment	World Fertilizer Use	Increment	Incremental Grain/Fertilizer Response Ratio
	(million metric tons)				(ratio)
1934-38	651		10		
1948-52	710	59	14	4	14.8
1959-61	848	138	26	12	11.5
1969-71	1,165	317	64	38	8.3
1979-81	1,451	286	113	49	5.8

*Annual Average for Period
Source: U.S. Department of Agriculture; United Nations Food and Agriculture Organization.

In many locations the demands on fisheries, forests and grasslands are becoming unsustainable. The world fish catch, which had tripled between 1950 and 1970, has increased little since then. During the twenty years before 1970 the fish catch increased nearly 6 percent per year, but since that year it has expanded at less than 1 percent per year.[31]

The deterioration of oceanic fisheries has been closely matched by the deterioration of the world's grasslands. After more than doubling between the early fifties and 1976, the growth in world beef production has come to a halt. With overgrazing now commonplace, the world's herders, farmers and ranchers find it increasingly difficult to

> "For the first time the World Bank is
> projecting a decline in living standards
> for a major region of the world."

23

expand their herds to match population growth. The result has been a steady decline in the world's per capita beef supplies since 1976 and stagnation in this subsector of the world agricultural economy.[32]

Just as diminishing returns are affecting food production, so too they are beginning to affect energy production. Efforts both to develop new petroleum resources and to more intensively exploit existing ones are experiencing diminishing returns. With a few notable exceptions, such as the South China Sea and the Arctic, the most promising prospects for discovering new oil fields have been thoroughly investigated.[33] Geological data indicate that new finds will be relatively meager and invariably located in more remote, inhospitable spots. In the Soviet Union, now the world's largest oil producer, Soviet official Gennardi Pisarevsky notes that, "Over the past 15 years the average pumping distance of one ton of oil in the U.S.S.R. has increased from 650 to 2,000 kilometers, by more than three times. Offshore drilling, which accounts for a substantial and growing share of the total exploration effort, can cost several times more per barrel than drilling on land."[34]

While the chances of discovering new oil grow smaller, the cost of pumping oil from older fields is climbing everywhere. Secondary and tertiary recovery techniques, which extract residual oil in older fields where conventional pumping no longer works, both cost more than primary methods and yield substantially less net energy. Commenting again on the Soviet Union, Pisarevsky reports that, "More than 10 percent of the production cost goes to maintain bed pressure: at present, 80 percent of the fuel is produced by pumping water, gas or air into the oil layers."[35]

In a world where the energy costs of producing everything are higher, the opportunities for savings are fewer and the competition for investment capital among sectors intensifies. As a result, investment capital is scarce and interest rates are high. In the absence of offsetting technological gains that develop cheap alternative sources, or that yield quantum jumps in energy efficiency, rapid growth becomes more difficult.

Between 1979 and 1982, the world economy expanded at less than 2 percent per year. Although these three years do not in themselves make a new trend, the less favorable resource conditions that contributed to the slower growth during these years may also lead to slow growth over the long term.

The *Wall Street Journal,* surveying European economic analysts at the end of 1982, reported that many saw the prolonged recession of the early eighties becoming permanent. In contrast to earlier recessions, when recovery translated into a 4 to 6 percent growth rate, the *Journal* noted that many European analysts saw recovery from the current recession in terms of 1 to 2 percent growth.[36]

For parts of the Third World prospects are even grimmer. Adebayo Adedeji, Executive Secretary of the Economic Commission for Africa, writes, "Not only are the forecasts for the immediate future gloomy, but the prospects for development and economic growth in Africa up to the end of the century are heart-rending. Indeed, if these projections are to be believed, the 1960s and 1970s may, by the end of the century, appear in retrospect to have been a golden age." Adedeji's assessment is matched by World Bank projections for Africa, which show a sustained decline in per capita income for much of the continent during the eighties. For the first time the Bank is projecting a decline in living standards for a major region of the world.[37]

Given the emerging constraints on growth, particularly in basic sectors such as food and energy, the world will have great difficulty resuming the rapid economic growth of the 1950-73 period. Under these more difficult circumstances, expanding global economic output even by an average of 2 percent per year may tax the skills of economic policymakers. With the prospect of much slower growth, countries with rapid population growth may face declines in living standards—unless they quickly slow their population growth.

Slower economic growth will affect all countries, but the effect will vary widely according to national population growth rates. For West Germany or Belgium, which have attained zero population growth, a 2 percent rate of annual economic growth will still raise incomes at 2 percent annually. For countries such as Kenya and Ecuador, with

"If an economic growth rate of 2 percent
per year becomes the new norm, nearly
half the world's people face possible
stagnation or decline in incomes."

populations expanding at more than 3 percent per year, a 2 percent
economic growth rate will produce steady declines in incomes and
living standards.

25

If an economic growth rate of 2 percent per year becomes the new
norm, then 2.1 billion people living in countries with population
growth rates of 2 percent or more per year, nearly half the world's
people, face possible stagnation or decline in incomes. Countries
where the threat of falling income is greatest are those where populations are expanding at 3 percent or more per year. This group of 29
countries, almost all in Africa, the Middle East and Central America,
have a combined population of 394 million.[38] Within this group,
countries with exportable surpluses of oil will be tempted to neglect
population policy, with the result that their populations will continue
to multiply rapidly, sustained with the imported resources financed
by oil exports. Over the long term, however, as oil reserves dwindle
and the exportable surplus disappears, these countries may find
themselves with populations that far exceed the carrying capacity of
local resources. Countries such as Iran and Nigeria, where oil production and exports have already peaked, illustrate well the risks that oil
producing countries with rapidly expanding populations face over
the long term. These countries are where the potential for catastrophe
is greatest.

Unfortunately, economic growth has already fallen behind population growth for many countries. The World Bank reports that per
capita GNP declined in 18 countries during the period from 1970 to
1979. (See Table 6.) In a few cases this was caused by disruption of
economic activity associated with political instability, but in the great
majority population growth simply outstripped growth in economic
output.

Given the prevailing economic conditions of the early eighties, the
ranks of the 18 countries with declining per capita GNP are likely to
swell dramatically. In a report published in late 1981 the World Bank
projected a decline in the average income of 24 low-income countries
in Sub-Saharan Africa with a total population of 187 million. For 11
other countries in Sub-Saharan Africa, all oil importing, low-income

Table 6: Countries Experiencing a Decline in Per Capita Gross
National Product, 1970-79

Country	Population	Annual Rate of Decline
	(millions)	(per cent)
Angola	6.9	-9.6
Bhutan	1.3	-0.1
Chad	4.4	-2.4
Congo	1.5	-0.2
Ghana	11.3	-3.0
Jamaica	2.2	-3.7
Libya	2.9	-1.6
Madagascar	8.5	-2.5
Mauritania	1.6	-0.7
Mozambique	10.2	-5.3
Nicaragua	2.6	-1.6
Niger	5.2	-1.2
Sierra Leone	3.4	-1.2
Uganda	12.8	-3.5
Upper Volta	5.6	-1.2
Zaire	27.5	-2.6
Zambia	5.6	-1.9
Zimbabwe	7.1	-1.7
Total:	120.6	

Source: *World Bank Atlas*, 1982.

developing countries, the Bank projected at best a standoff between
population growth and economic growth.[39]

Central to the decline in per capita income during the seventies in
many of the countries in Africa, a largely rural continent, was the
decade-long decline in per capita food production. The growth in

Africa's food supply compares favorably with that for the world as a whole, but its population growth is far more rapid. Plagued by the fastest population growth of any continent in history, as well as widespread soil erosion and desertification in the countryside, Africa's food production per person has fallen 11 percent since 1970.[40]

But as the growth in the production of material goods and services slows, the distribution issue must be viewed against a new backdrop, one unfamiliar to our generation. With the changing growth prospect, pressure to formulate economic and social policies with basic human needs in mind will no doubt increase even though it is far more difficult than it was in the era of rapid growth with its underlying theory that a rising tide raised all ships. As economist Herman Daly perceptively observes, turning our focus to meeting basic human needs will "make fewer demands on our environmental resources, but much greater demands on our moral resources."[41]

The Changing Population/Land Relationship

As the end of the oil age slowly draws nearer, concern with declining population/land ratios acquires a new urgency. The cheap energy that raised land productivity in so many ways after mid-century has now disappeared. With increases in the use of fertilizer, the principal yield-raising input, now yielding diminishing returns, shrinking cropland area per capita can threaten long-term per capita food production.

Declining supplies of oil not only make it more difficult to raise cropland productivity, but development of alternative energy sources will often exert new claims on cropland. In the past, population/land ratios influenced food production per person, but in the post-petroleum age, they will become one of the ultimate determinants of energy production per person. If population growth continues as projected, many countries may lack enough land to produce the energy needed to improve living standards.

Concern with the relationship between population growth and energy supplies is quite new, because world oil production until recently was expected to continue its long-term climb through the year 2000. Even when oil projections were revised downward after the first oil price hike in 1973, many thought that nuclear power would replace oil as the dominant global source of energy. But as the high cost of nuclear power became more apparent, it also became apparent that this energy source would never play more than a minor role in the world energy economy. In the United States, Wall Street has sounded the death knell for nuclear power by withholding the financial backing it needs to advance. Nuclear power is faring better in some countries than in the United States, and is doing worse in others. Overall, its future is not promising.[42]

The decline of oil has renewed interest in coal. But pollution problems caused by burning coal, including acid rain and increased atmospheric CO_2 levels, combined with finite reserves, mean that coal is only a transitional fuel. Synthetic fuels briefly held promise as a supplement to shrinking oil supplies. But most of the huge investments once slated for coal liquefaction and the development of oil shale and tar sands have been cancelled. As the eighties began, the United States, Canada, West Germany and Japan all had ambitious plans for commercial-scale synthetic fuel projects. Because of high costs and an uncertain technology, only a few projects remain.[43]

As the limited potential for nuclear power, coal and synthetic fuels becomes more evident, governments in both industrial and developing countries are counting increasingly on solar or renewable energy. Solar energy can be captured indirectly through forests, fuelwood plantations and energy crops. It can also be captured through mechanical devices such as rooftop solar collectors, photovoltaic cells, windmills, hydroelectric generators and through energy-efficient architecture.

Although renewable resources will help sustain economic growth, they will also compete for land. The challenge for policymakers is to devise energy development strategies that permit the growth in renewable energy to support improvements in living standards, as expanding oil output once did, without making unsustainable demands on the earth's land resources.

Some methods of harnessing solar energy require more land than others. Rooftop solar collectors that produce hot water offer little competition for land use. Growing energy crops to produce alcohol fuels, on the other hand, can compete directly with food crops.

29

In general, biological methods of energy collection consume more land than mechanical methods. In many Third World countries the demand for cooking fuel has already outstripped the sustainable yield of local forests. As a result, some villages have invested in intensively-managed firewood plantations, which produce more firewood than natural stands.

When wood is burned for both cooking and space heating, large areas of carefully managed natural forests or firewood plantations are required. In New England, where close to half of all homes now use wood to satisfy all or part of their space heating needs, a typical house can be heated with the sustainable yield from 1.5 hectares of woodland. (See Table 7.) New England has excess forest capacity with its current population, but such is not the case in most of the United States, or in most Third World countries.

A few developing countries have enough land to pursue a variety of renewable energy strategies. Brazil, with a pauper's endowment of fossil fuels and a once ambitious nuclear program in shambles, is building an industrial economy based almost entirely on renewable energy resources. Its program, aimed at largely eliminating oil imports by 1990, centers around development of its vast hydroelectric potential, the use of wood as a residential and industrial fuel and its rapidly advancing agriculturally-based alcohol fuels program.

Brazil is the world's leader in developing liquid fuels from agricultural crops. To become self-sufficient in automotive fuels, Brazil must plant sugarcane on an area of land close to half of that currently in crops. By the early eighties, well over a million hectares, some 4 percent of Brazil's cropland, had been planted to sugarcane for the production of alcohol. Fueling a Brazilian car with ethanol requires 1.1 hectares of sugarcane, roughly four times the average crop area per Brazilian. [44]

Brazil, which now relies on charcoal for 40 percent of its steel smelting, is also planting large areas to eucalyptus trees. Eventually, as the

Table 7: Area Required to Provide Domestic Energy Needs with Various Renewable Sources

Consumption Unit	Purpose	Fuel Source	Area
New England family	Residential space heating	Low grade and waste wood	3.6 hectares
New England family	Residential space heating	Sustainable yield of forest	1-1.5 hectares
Family, village in India	Cooking and domestic needs	Moderate-yield fuelwood plantation	0.5 hectares
Japanese family	Household hot water	Solar thermal panels	10 m^2
U.S. family	Household hot water with conventional backup system	Solar thermal panels	10 m^2
U.S. family	Domestic electricity needs	Photovoltaic array	30-50 m^2
Brazil	Annual fuel for 1 automobile	Ethanol from sugarcane	1.1 hectares

Source: Worldwatch Institute estimates derived from various sources.

wood for firewood comes less from natural stands and more from eucalyptus plantings, these plantations will occupy hundreds of thousands of hectares. With the fourteenth largest steel industry in the world, Brazil could become the first country with a modern steel industry primarily dependent on wood for its fuel.[45]

Brazil is also considering wood-derived methanol as a liquid fuel source. If eucalyptus trees are used to produce methanol, production of a thousand tons of methanol daily would require an estimated 72,000 hectares of new eucalyptus trees each year.[46] An auto fleet that could eventually run entirely on alcohol and a steel industry fueled by wood are easy options for a country that still has a relatively favorable population/land ratio.

Planning renewable energy strategies is not so easy for countries that are extravagant users of energy. In the United States, an ambitious program launched by the Carter Administration to produce two billion gallons of alcohol fuel from grain by 1985 (2 percent of the country's automotive fuel consumption) has fallen by the wayside. One reason is that expected oil price increases failed to materialize, making alcohol fuel production economically unattractive. But even if gasoline prices should double or triple, its economic feasibility would still be questionable given the low net energy yield of fuel alcohol produced from grain. Even if all the cropland in the United States were producing corn for conversion to ethanol, it would not provide enough fuel to satisfy current automotive fuel needs. To be successful, a U.S. effort to produce alcohol fuels from plants would probably depend on methanol from cellulosic materials.[47]

Not all biologically-based renewable fuels necessarily compete with other land uses such as food production. South Korea, for example, launched a program in the early seventies to reforest its largely denuded hillsides. With an area in village firewood plantations that is now roughly one-half the area planted to rice, this mountainous country has produced a major energy resource from unused land and seasonally unemployed labor. In this case, planting land to fast-growing pines did not compete with other land uses, and it reduced flooding and soil erosion and increased water conservation.[48]

Trees may produce energy cheaply, but mechanical devices generally require less land to collect energy. For example, solar collectors used to heat water can capture a third of the incident sunlight, while a field of high-yielding corn in the U.S. Midwest rarely converts more than 1 percent of the annual incident solar energy into biochemical energy. In the United States, residential hot water needs for a typical family can be largely satisfied with 60 square feet of solar panels. Moreover, these panels can usually be placed on rooftops where they do not compete with other uses. If fully exploited, this technology could satisfy much of the world's residential hot water needs without any important additional claims on land use.

Solar collectors for industrial use pose more land use problems than residential collectors. When industries use solar thermal panels to produce process heat in the form of hot water or, more commonly, steam, the area required is much larger and can often exceed the rooftop space of the industrial plant itself. In these cases additional land is needed near the plant, and a large industrial plant could easily require several acres of solar panels.

Photovoltaic cells, which convert sunlight directly into electricity, require a substantially larger area to satisfy home energy demands than solar thermal panels used solely for water heating. Photovoltaic cells are much less efficient, converting at peak just 10-12 percent of incident sunlight into electricity. But the area of photovoltaic cells needed to satisfy residential uses would not normally exceed the roof area of a single-family dwelling. Again, this method of collecting solar energy does not compete seriously with other land uses unless employed on a commercial scale. An electric utility in California, which is planning to generate 100 megawatts from photovoltaics, estimates that it will need 1,150 acres of photovoltaic cells, or roughly two square miles.[49]

Among the mechanically harnessed forms of renewable energy, one of the largest consumers of land is hydroelectric generation. In addition to claiming large areas of land, hydroelectric projects consistently produce conflicts because they lack flexibility in siting. Also, the best sites for hydroelectric dams and reservoirs are sometimes on river flood plains, land that is prime cropland. In addition to the conflicts with agriculturalists, dams often displace whole communities. Hydroelectric projects have also threatened wildlife preserves and local endangered species.

In Africa, Ghana built the huge Volta River project, leading to the creation of Lake Volta, even though the lake eventually inundated 8,500 square kilometers—an area nearly the size of Lebanon. The project also displaced thousands of villagers whose homes were inundated as the lake slowly filled. (See Table 8.)

Table 8: Land Area Covered by Large-Scale Hydro Projects

Project	River/County	Generating Capacity	Surface Area
		(megawatts)	(hectares)
Itaipu	Parana/Brazil-Paraguay	12,600	140,000
Tucurui	Tocantins/Brazil	7,960	146,000
Volta	Volta/Ghana	4,078	873,000
V. I. Lenin	Volga/USSR	2,300	650,000
Nasser	Nile/Egypt	2,100	525,000
Kariba	Zambezi/Zimbabwe	1,260	518,000
Kainji	Niger/Nigeria	836	128,000

Source: American Geophysical Union and various news articles.

To the east, China is considering construction of a mammoth dam at the Three Gorges site on the Yangtze River as it struggles to find the energy to modernize. Capable of expanding China's electric generation by nearly a third, the proposed project would inundate 45,000 hectares of cropland and require the resettlement of nearly two million people—no easy task in a country with a billion people already packed within its borders. Difficult though this will be, China may well proceed, consciously sacrificing cropland to gain the much needed energy.[50]

Specific examples illustrate the many ways hydropower competes with other uses of land. In India, a proposed dam in the state of Karnataka has been delayed since 1978 by owners of orchards. The dam would inundate 27,000 acres now planted largely to fruit trees. At another site in the state of Maharashtra, a 275-meter-high dam would submerge 23,000 hectares of prime teak forests. Local conservationists believe the teak, second in quality only to Burmese teak, is needed more than the additional hydroelectric capacity.[51]

34 As development of the earth's hydropower potential progresses, the share of the earth's land covered by water will slowly increase. Much of the land inundated by the projected doubling of world hydroelectric generation over the remainder of this century has no alternative use. But many projects will encroach on cropland, residential use or wilderness areas. As one of the largest renewable energy claimants on land, hydroelectricity can warn us of the growing competition for land between energy development and other uses.

Wind generators to produce electricity will also require large land areas, but this land can often be used simultaneously for other purposes. Some indication of land requirements for wind-generated electricity are now emerging in California, the world leader in developing wind electrical generation. Deudney and Flavin in their book, *Renewable Energy: The Power To Choose,* calculate that a thousand-megawatt power plant would require approximately 82 square kilometers of land devoted to windmills. The current goal of satisfying 10 percent of California's electrical demand with wind power would require some 615 square kilometers in wind farms. This would amount to 0.2 percent of the state's land area. Deudney and Flavin note that "wind rich countries should be able to get up to one-half of their electricity from wind machines that take up less than 1 percent of their land."[52]

Land used to generate wind power is often well-suited for grazing, forestry or even crop production. In California, ranchland leased for wind farms continues to be used to graze cattle. Wind-rich ranch land in the western Great Plains of the United States may one day be producing both beef and electricity.

A handful of countries have developed detailed plans for the renewable energy transition, including a detailed calculation of land requirements. Sweden, for example, projects that with no further population growth it could become essentially energy self-sufficient, relying largely on hydropower, fuelwood plantations and wind energy. With a relatively sparse population and with births and deaths

"To create a sustainable society in the
post-petroleum era, land everywhere
will have to be used much more
intensively and carefully."

already in balance, Sweden can make the transition to renewable
energy more quickly than most countries.[53]

Other countries developing long-term energy plans based heavily on
renewable energy are beginning to consider land requirements. For
example, under the ten-year energy development plan launched in
the Philippines in 1979 to reduce oil imports by 90 percent, energy
related activities will require nearly 3.5 million hectares of land,
440,000 of which will be in agricultural zones.[54]

35

Brazil could achieve liquid fuel self-sufficiency sooner and more easily
by relying less on the automobile and more on electrically-powered
urban and intercity rail systems. This would reduce liquid fuel requirements and lessen the competition for agricultural resources between transportation and food. Getting the brakes on population
growth will also help Brazil preserve its comparatively favorable
resource/population endowment that gives it so many energy options.

China, too, is moving vigorously to develop its renewable energy
resources—not so much because it lacks fossil fuels as because it lacks
the transportation infrastructure, investment capital and technologies
needed to exploit them fully. China's efforts have centered on the
construction of small-scale hydroelectric generators in rural areas, the
production of methane from organic wastes and an ambitious village
reforestation program designed to ensure a long-term supply of fuelwood. Alone, none of these decentralized energy sources will dominate this huge country's long-term energy picture, but together they
already dominate energy systems in rural China. Over the long term,
China can develop its largely untapped large-scale hydroelectric potential.

To create a sustainable society in the post-petroleum era, land everywhere will have to be used much more intensively and carefully. U.S.
agronomist R. Neil Sampson observes that, "Seldom has such a
totally new set of competitive forces been unleashed on the land as
those that appear on the horizon in the declining decades of the
petroleum era. As America and the world search for new sources of
industrial materials and fuels to replace increasingly expensive,

scarce or unreliable sources of the past, the major focus of attention has turned to agriculture."[55] As the pressures to intensify land use and create more jobs begin to multiply, so too will the pressures for land reform. Only by breaking up large holdings into small ones on which family labor can be applied intensively will it be possible to satisfy the many claims on agriculture, including those for jobs.

There are no comprehensive calculations currently available on the land required to support a world economy largely based on renewable energy sources. Among the unknown factors are the size of world population when it eventually stabilizes, the technological progress that will be made in increasing energy efficiency, and the particular technologies that will be used to harness solar energy in its many forms. The long-term decline in oil supplies and the growing demand for land to produce energy, however, are certain to make the relationship between population and land a key indicator of future economic health.

New Population Policies

As oil production declines, as biological systems deteriorate, and as the cropland area per person shrinks, economic growth is slowing. As it does, the nature of the population problem changes. In the past, rapid population growth slowed improvements in income, but for many countries, it now precludes them.

If future world economic growth averages closer to 2 percent than 4 percent, as now seems likely, then nearly half the world's people live in countries where population growth could exceed economic growth. In the absence of vigorous governmental efforts to brake population growth, the 121 million people living in countries where incomes fell during the seventies could multiply severalfold during the eighties.

This disturbing development is dividing the world into two groups: those where economic growth exceeds population growth, and those where it does not. For one group, living standards are rising. For the other they are falling. One group can hope that the future will be better than the present. In the other, hope is turning to despair as economic conditions worsen.

The fall in per capita incomes is occurring, almost without exception, in countries that have given little attention to the population side of the population/resources equation. Both the attention of political leaders and the allocation of budgetary resources have focused almost entirely on the supply side of the equation, on expanding output. One consequence of this imbalance is that more and more of the growth in output is required to satisfy the growth in population, with little remaining for improvements in per capita consumption.

Where population growth is rapid, changing economic circumstances call for new population policies. Traditionally, both industrial and developing countries have relied on the "demographic transition" to reduce their fertility. In the demographic transition, first observed in industrial Europe, early rises in living standards led first to declining death rates and then eventually, as incomes continued rising, to declining birth rates. The population equilibrium that existed in traditional societies when both birth and death rates were high was reestablished in modern society, but with low birth and death rates.

Many Third World countries have advanced far enough up the economic ladder that their death rates have fallen, but not far enough that birth rates have also fallen. According to demographer Michael Teitelbaum of the Ford Foundation, counting on the demographic transition to reduce fertility is "wishful thinking" by Third World governments since the modest level of development that most Third World countries hope for will not be sufficient to stabilize population size.[56] Fortunately, as some recent experiences show, countries with well-designed family planning programs that encourage small families can often bring fertility down even without the widespread economic gains that characterized the demographic transition in the industrial societies.

Countries where the growth in demand is approaching the sustainable yield of local biological systems may have to look beyond slowing the rate of population growth and take steps to halt the absolute increase in human numbers. For example, if the demand for firewood is nearing the sustainable yield of local forests, even a 10 percent increase in population and demand will lead to consumption of the resource base itself. In such situations, slowing population growth, though necessary and laudable, is not enough. Failing to halt population growth before the critical threshold is crossed will lead to fuel scarcities, fewer hot meals and a decline in the quality of life.

Governments with rapid population growth rates that wish to avoid a decline in living standards will need to reexamine their family planning programs. Making family planning services universally available helps curb population by preventing unwanted births. Although all governments represented at the U.N. Conference on Population in Bucharest in 1974 agreed that access to family planning services was a basic human right, not all governments have followed through.

Important though family planning services are, most countries will have to do far more. Reducing fertility to the level that circumstances seem to call for requires population education programs—designed not merely to acquaint people with family planning techniques, but also with the future relationship between population and resources. For the latter, China's experience is instructive. As part of a broad policy reassessment following Mao's death, the new leadership projected population and resource trends into the future. These projections were then used to launch public discussion of population policies and desired family size. Among other things, the projections showed that each Chinese currently subsists on scarcely one-tenth of a hectare, one of the smallest cropland allotments in the world, and that children and grandchildren can expect less still if population growth continues. Noting that even an average of two children per family would add another three or four hundred million people, the government used these population/resource projections to build support for the one-child family program.[57]

One result of these projections and their use in public discussion of population policy has been a shift in concern toward future generations. In China, as in most traditional societies, childbearing decisions were shaped by a desire by parents to be looked after in old age. By emphasizing future population/resource relationships in shaping family planning programs, government officials have shifted the fo-

"In an age of slower economic growth, improvements in living standards may depend more on the skills of family planners than on those of economic planners."

cus of childbearing from the well-being of parents to the well-being of children. Population/resource projections in other hard-pressed countries could play a similar role.

Against this changing economic backdrop many governments will need not only to help their people understand why population growth should be curbed quickly, but they can also begin developing various incentives and disincentives to do so. Each country can design its own package of economic incentives and disincentives, tailoring them to the values and interests of its people. Governments can reshape economic and social policies to encourage smaller families with population stabilization as a major social goal.

In many countries, reducing the birth rate rapidly enough to avoid a decline in living standards will require a herculean effort—the constant attention of national political leaders. Difficult though this may be, there have been some successes. Of the countries that have quickly reduced birth rates, China is both the largest and most well known. But it is by no means alone. In East Asia, South Korea and Taiwan, along with the city-states of Hong Kong and Singapore, have enjoyed remarkable success in reducing birth rates. With crude birth rates of 17, Singapore and Hong Kong are very close to the United States with a birth rate of 16. Within the Caribbean, Barbados and Cuba have birth rates of 17 and 14 respectively. Other countries with an impressive start in reducing fertility include Indonesia, Thailand, Colombia and Costa Rica. No two approaches are identical, but all involve a commitment to fertility reduction by the national government, the widespread availability of family planning services and educational programs that link population growth to the long-term social interest, as well as to benefits to individual families. Virtually all these countries also have used some combination of economic and social incentives or disincentives to encourage small families.[58]

Governments will be forced to settle differences between private interests, sometimes better served by larger families, and the public or social interests, better served by smaller families. Reconciling these differences can be extraordinarily complex. Failure, however, could be catastrophic. The issue is not whether population growth will eventually be slowed, but how. Can it be slowed humanely, through foresight and leadership, or will living standards deteriorate until death rates eventually begin to rise? A population equilibrium of sorts could be reestablished, but through high birth and death rates, rather than low birth and death rates.

In an age of slower economic growth, improvements in living standards may depend more on the skills of family planners than on those of economic planners. As the outlines of the new economic era become more visible, population policy seems certain to escalate on political agendas throughout the world. Too many countries have delayed too long in facing the issue. When they belatedly do so, they may discover, as China has, that circumstances will force them to press for a one-child family.

Notes

1. Worldwatch Institute estimates developed from annual growth rates reported by Wharton Econometric Forecasting Associates, Philadelphia, Penn.

2. The World Bank, *1981 World Bank Atlas*, (Washington, D.C.: 1982).

3. American Petroleum Institute (API), *Basic Petroleum Data Book*, Vol. 2, No. 3, (Washington, D.C.: September 1982).

4. U.S. Department of Agriculture (USDA), Economic Research Service, *World Indices of Agricultural and Food Production, 1950-81*, (unpublished, 1982).

5. United Nations Food and Agriculture Organization (FAO), *FAO 1977 Annual Fertilizer Review*, (Rome: 1978).

6. Motor Vehicle Manufacturers Association (MVMA), *World Motor Vehicle Data Book*, (Detroit, Mich.: 1982).

7. For aggregate and per capita growth rates for various commodities, see Lester R. Brown and Pamela Shaw, *Six Steps to a Sustainable Society*, (Washington, D.C.: Worldwatch Institute, March 1982).

8. U.S. Department of Energy (DOE), Energy Information Administration, *1981 International Energy Annual*, (Washington, D.C.: U.S. Government Printing Office, September 1982).

9. Japanese Ministry of Agriculture and U.S. Department of Agriculture, reported in Lester R. Brown, *Increasing World Food Output: Problems and Prospects*, Foreign Agricultural Economic Report No. 25, (Washington, D.C.: USDA, 1965).

10. FAO, *FAO 1977 Annual Fertilizer Review*, and Paul Andrilenas, USDA Economic Research Service, private communication, December 9, 1982.

11. Derived from USDA, *World Indices*, with population data from the United Nations Department of International Economic and Social Affairs Demographic Division.

12. *Ibid.*

13. Worldwatch Institute estimates from USDA, *World Indices*, and FAO, *1977 Fertilizer Review*.

14. FAO, *Production Yearbook*, (Rome: various years).

15. Harold F. Breimyer, "Preparing for the Contingency of Intense Pressure on Food-Producing Resources," Paper No. 1981-18, (Columbia, Mo: University of Missouri Department of Agricultural Economics, 1981).

16. Data on synthetic fibers from Textile Economics Bureau, *Textile Organon,* Vol. 53, No. 6, June 1982, and Robert Antoshak, Textile Economics Bureau, private communication, December 14, 1982. Cotton production figures from USDA, *Foreign Agriculture Circular* FC-12-81, May 1981, and FC-10-82, September 1982. Data on wool from John Lawlor, USDA, private communication, December 15, 1982.

17. Worldwatch Institute estimate based on data from FAO, *Production Yearbook,* 1981.

18. Christopher Flavin, *The Future of Synthetic Materials: The Petroleum Connection,* (Washington, D.C.: Worldwatch Institute, April 1980).

19. Raja Shahriman, Malaysian Rubber Bureau (Washington, D.C.), private communication, December 14, 1982.

20. World oil production data from API, *Basic Petroleum Data Book,* and *Oil and Gas Journal,* December 27, 1982.

21. *International Petroleum Encyclopedia 1980,* (Tulsa, Okla.: PennWell Publishing Co., 1980), and Workshop on Alternative Energy Strategies, *Energy: Global Prospects,* 1985-2000, New York: McGraw-Hill, Inc., 1977).

22. For example, see "The Changed Outlook for Petroleum," (interview with C. C. Garvin, Chairman and Chief Executive Officer of Exxon Corporation), *Oil and Gas Journal,* November 8, 1982.

23. The ups and downs of oil production in various countries during the seventies and early eighties can be traced in API, *Basic Petroleum Data Book.*

24. Erik Eckholm, *Losing Ground,* (New York: W. W. Norton & Co., 1976).

25. Raja Shahriman, private communication.

26. For a comprehensive review of world economic growth by country, with excellent commentary, see Herbert Block, *The Planetary Product in 1980: A Creative Pause?* (Washington, D.C.: U.S. Department of State, 1981).

27. MVMA, *World Motor Vehicle Data Book*

28. "A Land Use Policy for Canada," *Agrologist*, Autumn, 1975.

29. Lesley T. C. Kuo, *The Technical Transformation of Agriculture in Communist China*, (New York: Praeger, 1972).

30. USDA, *Foreign Agriculture Circular* FG-1-83, January 17, 1983.

31. FAO, *Yearbook of Fishery Statistics*, (Rome: various years).

32. FAO, *Production Yearbook*.

33. For a review of world exploration and new discoveries, see *Oil and Gas Journal*, December 13, 1982 (China), and January 31, 1983 (worldwide). An introduction to the geophysical aspects of offshore oil exploration may be found in "Oil and Gas Potential of the Maritime Boundary Region in Gulf of Mexico," *Oil and Gas Journal*, December 20, 1982.

34. Gennardi Pisarevsky, "The Search for Oil," *Soviet Life*, May 1980.

35. *Ibid*.

36. Debbie C. Tennison, "Europe is Adjusting to a Long Recession That Some Economists See as Permanent," *Wall Street Journal*, December 2, 1982.

37. Adebayo Adedeji, "A Gloomy Forecast for Africa," *IDRC Reports*, Vol. 10, No. 1, 1981; and The World Bank, *Accelerated Development in Sub-Saharan Africa: An Agenda for Action*, (Washington, D.C.: 1981).

38. Population Reference Bureau, *World Population Data Sheet*, (Washington, D.C.: 1982).

39. World Bank, *Accelerated Development in Sub-Saharan Africa*.

40. USDA, *World Indices*.

41. Herman Daly, in John Harte and Robert Socolow, eds., *The Patient Earth*, (New York: Holt, Rinehart and Winston, 1971).

42. For a concise overview of the nuclear industry worldwide, see *Financial Times Energy Economist*, No. 15, January 1983.

43. For an introduction to the prospects for synthetic fuels in North America, see "Uncertainty, Cost/Price Squeeze Hit Fledgling Synfuels Industry," *Oil and Gas Journal*, May 24, 1982, and "Alsands Tar Sands Project Terminated," *Oil and Gas Journal*, May 10, 1982.

44. Estimates of cane area required for alcohol production were derived from cane utilization statistics from Sam Ruff, USDA Economic Research Service, private communication, February 16, 1983. Estimate of cane area per automobile based on 1980 sugarcane yields, fermentation efficiency, and theoretical fuel requirements for a car fueled exclusively by ethanol.

45. A discussion of Brazil's charcoal consumption for steel smelting in the context of overall wood demand is included in FAO, *Tropical Forest Resources,* FAO Forestry Paper no. 30, (New York: UNIPUB, 1982).

46. For a concise review of the methanol and ethanol options, see William Ramsey, "The Alcohol Fuels Option in the Third World," *The Energy Journal,* Vol. 2, No. 1, 1981.

47. U.S. Congress, Office of Technology Assessment (OTA), *Energy from Biological Processes,* (Washington, D.C.: U.S. Government Printing Office, July 1980) provides an exhaustive overview of biomass technologies and policy choices, particularly in the U.S.

48. Erik Eckholm, *Planting for the Future: Forestry for Human Needs,* (Washington, D.C.: Worldwatch Institute, February 1979).

49. Christopher Flavin, *Electricity from Sunlight: The Future of Photovoltaics,* (Washington, D.C.: Worldwatch Institute, December 1982).

50. "More dam news . . .", *World Environment Report,* February 15, 1983.

51. "Opposition Delays Indian Dam 4 Years," and "More on Hydro-Power," *World Environment Report,* December 15, 1982.

52. Daniel Deudney and Christopher Flavin, *Renewable Energy: The Power to Choose,* (New York: W. W. Norton & Co., forthcoming).

53. Thomas B. Johansson and Peter Steen, *Solar Sweden,* (Stockholm: Secretariat for Future Studies, 1978).

54. Philippine Ministry of Energy, *Ten Year Energy Program, 1980-89,* (Manila: 1980).

55. R. Neil Sampson, "Energy: New Kinds of Competition for Land," presented to the 35th Annual Meeting of the Soil Conservation Society of America, Dearborn, Mich., August 6, 1980.

56. Quoted in Jeremy Cherfas, "The World Fertility Survey Conference: Population Bomb Revisited," *Science 80*, November 1980.

57. "11m Chinese Opt for 'Only Child Glory Certificate'," *People* [Journal of the International Planned Parenthood Federation], Vol. 9, No. 4, 1982.

58. For an overview of efforts to reduce fertility, see *People*, Vol. 9, No. 4, 1982, and W. Parker Maudlin, "The Determinants of Fertility in Developing Countries: An Overview of the Available Empirical Evidence," *International Family Planning Perspectives*, September 1982. Individual country reviews have been published in various issues of *Population Bulletin*, Population Reference Bureau, Washington, D.C.

45

LESTER R. BROWN is President of and a Senior Researcher with Worldwatch Institute. Formerly Administrator of the International Agricultural Development Service of the United States Department of Agriculture, he is the author of several books, including *World Without Borders*, *By Bread Alone*, *The Twenty-Ninth Day*, and *Building a Sustainable Society* (W.W. Norton, October 1981).